COMING UP FOR
Light and Air

POEMS
Barbara Crow

Minnesota Voices Project Number 67

New Rivers Press 1995

New Rivers Press is a non-profit literary press dedicated to publishing the very best emerging writers in our region, nation, and world.

The publication of *Coming Up for Light and Air* has been made possible by generous grants from the Dayton Hudson Foundation on behalf of Dayton's and Target Stores, the Jerome Foundation, the Metropolitan Regional Arts Council (from an appropriation by the Minnesota Legislature), the North Dakota Council on the Arts, the South Dakota Arts Council, and the James R. Thorpe Foundation.

Additional support has been provided by the Bush Foundation, the General Mills Foundation, Liberty State Bank, the McKnight Foundation, the Minnesota State Arts Board (through an appropriation by the Minnesota Legislature), the Star Tribune/Cowles Media Company, the Tennant Company Foundation, and the contributing members of New Rivers Press. New Rivers Press is a member agency of United Arts.

New Rivers Press books are distributed by The Talman Company, 131 Spring Street, Suite 201 E-N, New York, NY 10012 (1-800-537-8894).

Coming Up for Light and Air has been manufactured in the United States of America for New Rivers Press, 420 N. 5th Street/Suite 910, Minneapolis, MN 55401. First Edition.

For Jay

For Liz, Melanie, Sarah and Jeff,
Alice and Mark

In memory of
Jonathan

ACKNOWLEDGMENTS

The author is very grateful to Mark Vinz for his early encouragement, and she thanks all the members of *Wordshop*, in Fargo, and *Other Voices*, in Grand Forks, for their suggestions and love, without which there would be no *Coming Up for Light and Air.* Thank you to Sandy Krom, whose patience and good humor in typing this manuscript was a balm. And thank you to Geoff Tidmarsh for allowing her to feature a photograph of his sculpture "Woman, Child, & Seal," done by Mary Ezekiel. Warmest thanks to editor, Bill Truesdale, and to Katie Maehr and Michelle Woster, staff of New Rivers Press, for their enthusiasm and empathy. Lastly, she has a debt of gratitude to her husband, Jay, whose love was the catalyst for this book.

Some of the poems in this collection originally appeared in the following publications, sometimes in slightly different forms: *A Circle of Four* (Dacotah Territory Press), *Clearing Space, Dust and Fire, Half Tones to Jubilee, Poets On, Prairie Volcanoes,* and *Red Weather.* Our thanks to the editors for allowing us to use the poems here.

Half Tones to Jubilee, a journal published by Pensacola Junior College, awarded "Hands" first place in the Fourth Annual Poetry Contest in 1992.

"Crusoe's Canoe" is from *The Entrance To Purgatory* by Iain Lonie, published by John McIndoe, Ltd. Used with permission.

The Bone People by Keri Hulme was published by Hodder Headline. The quote is used with permission.

The front cover artwork, entitled *Zhao Bing of the Later Han,* one of sixteen paintings on silk from the album *Keepsake from the Cloud Gallery,* is in the collection of the British Library in London. It is used with permission.

CONTENTS

"I will always be a wanderer.
Such is my nature."

— Jonathan's journal

I

Te mutunga—ranei te take = the end—or the beginning

TRANSLATION FROM MAORI
The Bone People
—Keri Hulme

THE FIG TREE

Green is returning
to the fig tree, flushing like new blood
through thin brown stems.

Last winter,
I gave up all hope
for this tree.

Early summer,
and I put the plant
on the patio
where it bathes
in light
and rain.

Every day
I go out and inspect
new buds, tiny leaves,
and right now, as I lie
on the deck chair—
it's dusk and I'm reading
Maxine Kumin—I look beside me
and feel good
having saved this one dumb life.

Entering In

I took the ring from my finger
this morning. I'm thriving.

I'm reading love poems. Last month,
last year, all I could swallow

was death. My husband closes doors
quietly, but I hear tiny bells

on his feet as he leaves. Are all days
like this? I sit in a state of grace

in the chair, spilling out my life for
this woman. Listen, I say,

my whole body
leaning towards her, towards

the light that heaves itself into the room.

Genesis

This is where the hard loving began,
here at the bay's final sweep, partly

hidden from shore by rocks and a wooden
device for showering.

It wasn't here ten years ago.
Not much else was either. Just these

old dry hills and the sea
and you. Well, my darling, the pure

pull for the south is gone, and all
that is left are these

signs to swim out from the island.

Tonight, having dined for the second
evening on chicken breasts in wine sauce,
rice, brown and sweet, and lettuce dubbed
with Roquefort, casting off the mantle
of despair, I'm entering into hope, I mean,
waking up to a new poem, lines
popping in and out of my mouth while I
shake with love and this other thing I've known
for years is happiness, like the morning
I walked the docks at Onehunga, leaving the bed
of a man I didn't love, heading home,
sky clearing, all things coming clean.

I'm surprised that my hands are still dark.
I could unfold each one, but, don't. What is it

we've done, this separation of bone
from flesh, the way skin leaves us? Once,

in the island, I fell upon sand. We had entered
a cave. He lit a fire and stood looking

out to sea. Rain, aqua, and words stronger
than we had known. Now, my daughter writes

of the *strongest* wind. Someone says,
no, *wind* is all you need. I tell her,

believe in the one that comes to you
without hesitation, cleaving to you

bone to pared bone, grafted
cleanly without shade or light.

BENEDICTION

This morning,
I sit at the breakfast table

where the lit candle stands
upon the white cloth,

where the poetry
manuscript I have set apart

waits on the wooden
table, pure

parchment telling me
all that it is

I have been trying
to decipher—

the whereabouts
of you,

this space
you have entered.

JOURNEY BACK

The night train halted
time after time by rain
and mud slips, things
coming unhitched

all along the line,
we miss the ferry,
so take the inter-island
flight over the Straits,

a rocky crossing.
Then, it's the Daylight Express
down the coast, and we're speeding
home. All windows open

for the cold sea air,
it's late when we pull
into the plains, into
the arms of aunts,

brother, sisters, and the new
dark space that is everywhere.

EVIDENCE

All the tracks you took me on, striding
ahead of me through the forest till we came

to the startling view of the sea,
the inlet where you told me about an Indian

ghost seen paddling his canoe,
the evidence found on the beach, later.

In your apartment now, we stand
by your futon as it was the hour

you left it. On the window-sill
in sun, one perfect sand-dollar,

and your clock, stopped
at nine-thirty. Around the room,

your clothes, freshly-laundered,
folded, neat.

I want to put your sneakers
together, but find

only one, and then remember
what they told us, that you had on

one sneaker and one hiking boot
when they found you,

where you fell.

SON

at the mortuary
we wait

in a room
as dim as this

new image of you,
the you no longer

tall, no longer
walking. how far

we traveled
to be

where you
were.

INHERITANCE

Late for your funeral, the hard drive
from Seattle in the rain
to find the black hearse
gone. It was alright,
you, going on
ahead as usual.

And then,
the cemetery,
stepping out into light,
the walk to the canopy gripping
the hands of your friends,
those who loved you
or endured you, all of us
accepting what we didn't want,
this gift you'd bequeathed,
the weight of you
beginning
to settle.

AT THE CATHOLIC CEMETERY

we stand around your grave
holding hands, the earth

swollen and waiting.

Sharing you now with others, news
of you and your death, wanting to pull
many into mourning, a kind of
rebirth perhaps, because if I stop
talking about you, will you be
truly gone. This awful

rush to get you in print, have you
etched somewhere apart from
the granite stone that says,
so formally and unlike you,
the dates of your birth
and death, the words
Beloved Son,
a cross on one side,
the yin-yang symbol
on the other.

Your father chose that symbol,
drew the marker with a steady
hand that day at the funeral home,
and I said, But I don't
like that. And he stood firm.
Later, in your apartment
above your futon, we saw
your drawing of this
circle with two small
moons inside, one black,
one white, for all the dark
and all the light
in the light and dark
of all of us.

BREATHING SPACE

a hot summer night.

on a hill
somewhere else,

an owl flies the perimeter
of his territory,

singing.

FLIGHT

Over the ocean, somewhere
between Hawaii and Fiji, it came to me

that my mother was utterly gone. I was flying
home for her funeral. Outside, clouds

dispersed. We're actually parting air,
I remember thinking. Far to my left,

there's the horizon, the very lip
of our finite universe. Always,

on this journey, the minute I see
that straight, clean line, I'm the first

voyager, the bell-ringer, the heralder
of a truth: I'm nearly home,

the life I've taken in America
passing into obscurity, to be remembered

on occasion as a puzzle, or bit of one,
an engraving brought out for private

showing, but rarely missed,
even in sleep. I fly on to Aotearoa,

a plate of soft scrambled eggs and mangoes
on my lap. I'm breakfasting

in the Southern Hemisphere, and a Fijian
islander is gliding towards me,

extending his golden arm
like a sign, a burnished offering.

AT HECLA ISLAND

We came for the arctic air,
or whatever kind of pure mass
pulls a people from city streets
to here, where

right now, we're walking the boards
over swamp and bullrushes,
dragging ourselves out of

thin reeds, rising like
goshawks into blue frightened air.

today, in this wide light land

i stop

in the middle of unloading

groceries, gifts,

wine—our twenty-fifth

wedding anniversary—

take myself outside in the cold dakota air

and breathe in

for you.

I watched you,
that day on the patio,

your head bent under the weight
of the pressing in your lungs,

your whole body
moving with every breath.

I could do nothing
but sit and breathe with you.

When I saw that spider
rappelling down the geranium stem,

its sharp black legs
traversing peaks and boulders,

I wanted to show you,
but it was clear you were entering

far more difficult territory.
And then the spider

scuttled into the dark
of the undergrowth

and I couldn't see it anymore.

In Aotearoa

Your body was taken
and washed, then

the midnight trip
home by hearse, the indelicate

tipping of you into bed.
Nobody went into your room

after that. I slept
on the floor, woke early

and sat in your kitchen
drinking tea and reading poems.

Every now and again
I'd go to the window, hungry

for the sounds of morning—
tuis and bellbirds and trains

running off to the hills.
I couldn't get enough

of the big wet stars,
the way night was moving

out of itself. And then
the sun came dripping

all over frost,
and little tufts of grass

were trying to spring up.

VISITATION

After Mother's death,
my brother writes of his new home.
He can see sandhills from the front window,
hear the sea when the wind comes
from the east.

Birds gather daily out the back,
line up on the brick wall.
"I think they must want to be fed,"
he writes.
"The old chap who lived here
must have fed them."

"What should I do?"
he asks.

I write back,
"Feed them, for heaven's sake.
Don't you know who it is?
Can't you tell,
the way they start
early in the morning
and won't let up

till you go out
and let the sun
break on your cold grey face?"

Winter schedules come
daily now. Flat
offerings like

the shape of this land.
Little moves me.

I examine
the plight
of an elder bug

trapped. Then
think of bear,
go out,

push back
the flank of snow
and wrap the cap

of earth around me.

Coming Up for Air

The day a madman shot the judge
in the local county courthouse,

I lost my mind. Amnesia:
a laying down of arms, a sudden

tip in the cerebral axis, events
collapsing into each other

like box-cars on the railway line,
a brain, disengaged,

on the run. Think of it
this way—a body, dormant too long, so

an uprising, rebellion in the caverns,
cells slipping past sentries, passing

wrist upon wrist up a long shaft of light.

You wanted a shower,
so you came to my room,
that morning in Olympia,
the shower you had
hardly a trickle
of cold water
from a rubber hose
on a tap.

You came out singing,
emerging
a fresh new thing,
crooning to yourself
in the mirror, brushing back
your thick tawny hair,
wailing to the you
that grinned back—
"You are so beautiful
to m e e e e,"
letting go of that vowel
till it sounded like
some new kind of animal
taking refuge
in my room.

Visitor

The guest bedroom is ready.
All morning I scuttled

in and out the wooden door
carrying fresh white sheets,

starched cloths, plumped up
pillows frothy with lace.

Someone must be coming
over the prairie sea needing

bread and a place to sleep.
I wait

all day. The wind rises.

ANNIVERSARY

This first cold
fall day, my husband

took me to the wildlife
refuge. We climbed

to the top of the lookout;
saw one grey heron

hiding in weeds,
and, far in the west,

a slew of geese
circling, landing,

crying, firm white
wings slashing air.

All day I hear their
pure, insistent

ring.

After a Good Dream about My Son

In this dream, we were on a train journey,
and you were at the helm, only

it wasn't you, in the way of dreams—
chaos and order, a sudden

departure from the tracks, the quick, grim
threat of falling; a cliff,

and a sheer drop. But things righted
and became stable, your father

at the helm, for a while. And then,
it was you, your day; flags like celebratory

wings in the sky. You were wearing
your old white shirt, the one you wore

for your high school graduation photo,
and I was clapping and patting your back,

enthralled to have you with us, alive
and hearing. And in the dream,

and later on waking,
I could hardly believe my good fortune.

SONG

The morning after the good dream
about my son,

I sit in the blue velvet chair
in the living-room,

going through old *New Yorker* poems.
I keep some,

toss the rest. They lie,
clean white

rags on the floor.
I've been here

a long time now,
listening to a flute

clearing the morning air.

CLEARING SKY

A white cloth is now
on the table by the door.

All day I've been cleaning,
looking for the kind of magic

that will pull my tent
clear up to the sky.

This table could be
an altar: a candle,

one blue bowl with
two birds flying over

clouds, my white lamp
with ravens singing

on a bough of blossom,
and above all this,

the framed collection
of photos from Mendocino

of trees on the cliffs
and surf and rocks.

It was high noon
and full sun when we

sat there eating
Italian flatbread,

looking out to sea.

Gulls were circling the stone wall
at the bottom of the garden,

and lupins flattened themselves
against barbed wire the day

the storm swept in from the sea.
In the house in Timaru,

your names were spoken—
Jonathan, Sarah,

Melanie, Liz, and Alice.
But Jonathan was not there.

Death had taken
the first of you.

MY DAUGHTERS HAVE THEIR OPERATIONS

Twice I've entered with my daughters
into this kind of sleep. In the green
waiting-room, I've held their hands
as they stretched for the arms
of the medicine-man. When they rise

up from sleep, we talk
in low voices of the men who've
left us, the ones we loved
and lost, the ones we thought
we'd never get over.

I tell them,
there was this man once.
I thought I would
die if he left me. And something
breaks through for us as I
bend to scan their small
red scars,
kiss the fur on their tiny hands.

Travelers

Coming out of the forest to the lake at last,
the long hike over, water stretching before us,

we sail north—floating, moving
swiftly and easily, like the loon

and the eagle, and the bear
that entered our tent later

leaving soft wet
paw marks on canvas,

no footfall heard.

It's the first good summer morning
and I'm driving into Minnesota.

Where I'm heading
no one else seems to be.

At a crossroads, I sense
a change in direction,

like birds must feel
when they leave

one land for another.
I turn and veer north,

running the old glacial
highway, looking for signs,

wanting things to spring
up from the dust.

CONSORT

I saw the wind moving through the grass
this morning. And then three crows rose

up into air. I'm always looking for signs.
Last night, I slept in a bed free of fur,

so clean, I could have been floating
on the belly of a woman. I dreamed

of Prince Charles and his Diana. They were
to meet the Queen, but reluctant, so

I was consort—she who guides the soul
between worlds. The Queen was beaming.

"Go to her," I said to Charles, all the time
aware it was Diana who needed help, a word,

something more than a wooden arm around
her waist. That was the dream. In this life,

I'm sitting in a booth in a Danish restaurant
telling things, but not all things. We've finished

our eggs and sausage. I'm done with the clean
smart life. The sun heavy on my face, it's with

pure joy I go out into the wind, step on the gas
and head south into prairie.

It's June the twenty-fourth,
and you've been dead three years this day.

Sun

How warm the pink cushion is
upon the chair. I've spent

all my pennies. Wine, potent,
magical, floats me. In the mail

today—a fine poetry book.
It inspires me. I cook

brown rice, add ginger,
garlic, sesame oil and mushrooms,

then open shades and walk
through rooms

I thought I could not enter.

Given Two Hours

We'll buy books of poems
and live on them. In the store,

I ask my daughter—
a poet—so, what do you think

of his poems? I offer the whole book
to her, but it takes off, rises

up from my hands, flies, pages
spilling, and lands at her feet.

I pick up pages, hungry,
my hair lifting into light.

Where did they come from,
these babies that sprang
from my body? Some days
I hardly know them,
though I remember
when they left me, swimming
like tadpoles
from my belly,
my breast.

Now, I'm leaving them.
Miles past the point
of no return,
having taken each one, alive
or dead, in my arms
and blessed them,
I am going on.   With others,

in the way things do,
massed for travel,
we swim out to the island.
And I think that it's not
a strange thing, none of us
wanting to talk or look back,
not wanting to know
if the young are swimming well,
if their fins are big enough,
the current for them
or against them.

II

You have to let things die
in their own gentle way

to sail off from the island.

—Iain Lonie
"Crusoe's Canoe"
from *The Entrance To Purgatory*

In This Room

My mother lies
on the iron bed.

The moon dips into the room.
It is late to come.

I sit in the chair by the bed
and watch my mother,

a curl of bone
between sheets.

The fan is on low.
It has such slow arms.

Its small winds play
with her hair. It's

fine now, her hair,
and thin. This wind

wants to love it.
I think this wind

wants to carry it away.

PLAINS WOMAN

I remember hearing about your brothers,
the seven who kept you, for a season,
from your love, guarded you in church
and town by linking arms around you.
And I heard how you found a way
and met this man, here in the garden
among the glistening plums.

I don't know what happened
to the brothers or the man.
Nobody talks of these things.
But this is a house gone
dry with sun, and washing still hangs
in the blue-gum trees.

It's full summer.
Little dragonflies are offering themselves
to the rocks, and sheets
belonging to your own people are
slapping in the warm wind
sweeping up from the plains.

EASTER

The daughters are coming
home for Easter, bringing friends.

It'll be good to have song
in the house again, and talk

of poetry and writing. Watch
my silver girls, my three blonde

Indians sparring for a place
at my side, slipping about

in their new, wet skins.

Out at the farm today,
trailing your father as he tills the land,
I take your place and look for stones,
arrowheads, trinkets, things
buried and now risen, making my usual
bargain with God for some rare find
to tell me you're alive and hearing.

It's good to be here, the day
sunny, the wind strong and hard.
I like to feel dry clods
break under my bare feet as I pick up
stones, warm from hours of sun,
and duck's eggs split
wide open, their small inhabitants
gone.

At the end of the field,
I find slivers of iron and a shard
of porcelain, white, with a crown design
barely visible, and I wonder if
this is where the settlers had their hut
and were massacred. I think of the braves
slipping in by night, perhaps it was supper,
they came swinging in to do what they
had to do, break plates and bodies
as if each were a part of the other.
I don't want to hear that these are
recent discards. I'm set on tired immigrants
finding water at last and a place to
stop for the night, Grandma's
plate from Bristol set out for bread.
I feel this tiny piece of it, feel
its sharp edge and suddenly,
I want your father, I want him
to stop working and come to me.

I look up and see him
far in the west,
big and raw with love for you,
still tilling.

FEAST DAY

Your father's birthday, and we dine
on salmon in kickapoo sauce, Greek salad,

dark sweet olives and tart cheese.
It's the chocolate decadence dessert

that stays with me for hours. I vow
I won't eat again; fear the loss

of such rich moistness, press my tongue
to the roof of my mouth, hard,

willing taste buds to bring back
all the sweetness of raspberry sauce

lying pooled on the white china plate
like warm, thick blood.

Sabbatical

The sun is making patterns on the wood. It's also
on my back. Inside, the white cat sleeps, sprawled

legs flung south, nose to the north. I left my china
cup on the table, and the camera, too. A while ago,

I took this photo which I'll title: "What I see on a Sunday
morning sitting on the patio,"—sneakers, and gardening clogs

sidling together by the railing; two *North Dakota Quarterlys*
brought out for cerebral refreshment. Now, a lawn-mower

starts up. I can actually smell the perfume of these
petunias and the wood. A bee drums by me. I keep thinking

of going inside to get a glass of water. But,
my legs ache, and my head's just coming right, and I don't

even know who I am this Sunday morning, legs askew
under the hot pink cotton dress, straw hat

blazing my head, my back to the sun,
sweet air spreading for miles.

An errant bubble
as I wash dishes today
comes rising
up from the sink
as I fan it
this way
and that,
shooing it
far from all sharp
edges, all dangerous, hard things.

And I start to laugh,
it's so feisty,
can't take my eyes off
how easily it floats,
lifts
higher. I
breathe it
away, all wet and glistening
and swimming through air.

FAR COUNTRY

for Deb

On all journeys now I mourn, but
today, on this long drive south,

it's something more. From the moment
I saw your writing on the letter

in the mail-box this morning,
all loss has catapulted into this

one fresh absence—you, no longer
here. These days, I take what I can,

the balm of your voice over the wires,
and this thing I can't quite find

words for—how, when I saw your writing
on the yellow envelope, it was as if

my own name had been carved
into the bark of a tree, or on a stone

in a country I cannot envision.

At Voyageurs National Park

Sailing across Lake Kabetogama,
sun and spray for miles,

it comes to me—the sudden knowledge that
this is where my ashes will be strewn.

I've been heading here
all my life, since days I stood

on the antarctic shelf looking
out, feeling the first

stirrings of new thin
limbs like cricket wings.

I've found the burial waters.

Now, faces to the wind,
we speed over warm

waves of light, leaving behind
the subterranean land,

the kingdom of darkness beautifully on hold.

BOY

In New Zealand,
swimming the Takaka rapids,
you told Cousin Katie,

"Do it," she'd be alright,
you knew. And when she
jumped in, found the current
strong and dangerous and yelled,
"Where will it take us?"

you said, laughing
as you swept past her,
"Don't know,
never done this before."

YOUR WHOLE YOUNG BODY

Your fresh handwriting leaps
out at me from the box

under my bed, a collection
of your letters

forgotten about,
bringing a grave new

affirmation of your death.
What they tell us

of your whole young body
is so far removed from

what we have. Coda.
This forever

absence of you.
Unlike that sea urchin

stuck with a needle
at the seminar in California,

spurting out
cells to be impregnated

that we watched
divide and divide

and divide;
your progeny,

all the divisions
of you—

cancelled.

PICNIC AT THE RIVER

You wanted to take me on a picnic,
that last weekend in Olympia,
and made sandwiches, thick slabs
of white bread with cold lamb
and tomatoes, packed this old-fashioned
lunch-box like I did for you
as a child. You wanted to show me
this river where the water is clear
and flows swiftly like the rapids
you swam in New Zealand.

I drove, and you sat beside me, twiddling
the radio knob, singing, and slapping your knee.
You gave me directions to get
out of town, but what happened next
is mystery: I drove
to the river without any help
from you. It was as if the car had
taken over, and instinct, too.
We left the highway,
passed the Catholic Cemetery,
and the strange thought
came to me as we neared the river,
that you had not told me how to get there
and I had not asked you; I just
got us there in that foreign territory
with no help from you.

We skipped stones, flat grey
stones across the water, and walked
some distance down the length of it.
This great sadness came over me.
I couldn't shake it. I left you
and walked through bush, looking
up at the sky, looking
for answers I would not have believed.

What it is I do not say

Something I want to put
down on paper, but I fear

what it is I do not say,
the words not spoken.

Coming in from the cold,
putting down the bowl

I've carried for so long
from that other house

to this, I want you to know,
on that long passage out,

I couldn't stop looking at the sky.

I wanted to break
in the night, take it

like a lover,
a spare skin,

a black
body glove,

the darkness
of this long Dakota night.

HANDS

The thing is, I want to put
lotion on my hands. Before the doctor
saw them yesterday, the priest prayed
over the cracks and holes, fissures
in palms bleeding. "Oh, Lord," he said,
"What is it You have for these hands
to do?" So I need lotion.
But I'm not thinking about my hands
right now. I'm thinking about what it is
I really want to say, how I can't stop reading
this poem in *The Paris Review.* It's a sestina,
six stanzas, six lines, thoughts, phrases
rearranged all through, and it's about a woman
who sees a deer on her way to work.
Great Dane! she keeps saying in this poem,
and I'm struck with the flow,
the movement, how the reader (meaning
me) is taken out to a road on a hill
through a forest. It's in Minnesota,
pine and spruce, and the last thing
the woman in this poem is thinking of
is a deer crossing her line of vision,
coming into it with a bang.
Oh God, she says, and Great Dane!
and, How far we have come. And I think
of great poems read at odd times, how they
come to mind and won't leave, poems
out of the blue, like another one about
a man in Montana standing on a butte one night,
a still winter night. The moon
full, he looks downwind and hears a braying
coming from the river below and what he sees
will drive him crazy for the rest of his life,
a wolf, stranded on an ice floe,
standing, crying on an ice floe
on a river in Montana, and this man
on a butte on a clear
cold night watching.

Like artifacts from some far country,
your tin spoons glitter
when we empty your pack.

It's what is left
for us, this rude
division of your goods,
the sacrament performed
without you. Gently

we pick at what
you held. I take
the pack to the basement,
know how it will
greet me every time I go
down, your bright orange
glowing
like a beacon
on the concrete floor.

Good Fortune

I thought it would trail you,
all your life. You were the good luck child.
Swimming the bottomless lake, your mother
ahead, her lazy breast-stroke opening up
water for you, but weeds reaching
tangled your legs until your father came
cleanly through wet green foliage,
freeing you. And the time you took
the mountain trail fast so fast,
rising over the world and
surviving. It's fear

I fear more than death, the part before
dying when suddenly
it's inevitable, and you'll know it,
like that brief catch of breath
the moment before the tumble
into a glacial kind of peace
and light will break for you
and you'll be eight again
swimming the forbidden lake,
Father rising out of water
like Poseidon coming
floating, carrying you in his arms.

Entering Air

Coming down from the mountains,
I turned when I saw
cottonwoods on a hill,

and put my palms to my belly
when the beating of feathers
began. The bird in my body

was growing, its wings
lengthening. Nobody could tell me
about migration, why some birds

go south, and some north.
I didn't know then, how a bird could ever

leave such a moist nest
to enter the dry air,
nor how empty it would be

inside my body.

HEALING

I read Naomi Nye's essay
on William Stafford,

and Kim Stafford's words
about getting up

early to lie where his father
had lain, and then

I pick up this paper
and finish the poem

about your body
and what happened to it

lying all day in the sun.

DREAM

It's enough to be
looking north today.

The road west
has lost its lure.

Even south
is a forgotten land.

I think of our trip
through inland

waters, prairie
reeds, birds rising

out of rushes
like princes in a dream.

At Agassiz Sanctuary

Images of fish float through me,
little live orange fish

like minnows in technicolor.
At the refuge yesterday,

the lake's ice broken,
water swollen, filling

pools on the road,
we watched tiny fish trapped,

darting into wet grass.
Your father bent down

and rescued one after the other,
picking up their soft

flopping bodies, putting them
back into the coulee.

All day walking in the arctic air,
I dream we're saving you.

WORDS

What to say when people ask
how many children do we have?

I won't let go of you,
tell them your name,

and where you are now,
add, almost always,

that you were bright
and beautiful,

as if this would negate
that you died

which has become
the largest fact

about you.

At the End of the Bay

Signs were there, all along,
in your talk of migration

to the land that was calling you.
And the morning I watched you

at Takatu, swimming
to the end of the bay, coming

out of water like some
luminous sea god. Later,

walking back up the track,
the moon drained your face,

and I saw, with no great
astonishment, that you had

become your own ghost,
leaving me this new way, lightly

sifting through me with your warm
and sun-bleached bones.

AFTER YOUR DEATH, YOUR LETTER COMES

And I think, as I take
and place it, warm

and folded, of the way
we'll go on reaching

back, the wild rushing
journey through bone

to your body's quiet
collection of bone and hair.

And I love how it lies
in that great almond sheet

and I love that we took you
down to the sea and

placed you there, light
cancelling everything from us

here on out that hour
in the street of stones, villagers

echoing what we chose
to sing over you

at the edge of the field
and its shining hedge.

LOVING THE SEAL-WOMAN

I'm so hungry for books, words, things that
imprint themselves on me. Sam Hamill says
a wind over waves
cools little sandcrabs washed up
along the beach, and I
praise such a man,
want to take him
whole, swallow all he has
to say. I have this great
attachment for his lines, his way
of grafting words. This day,
walking slowly and with
an awful deliberation over concrete
paths, stopping
once, to gawk at sky
and birds, I see
three crows
tearing up off a grey slab
stone that could be a marker
for a grave. I think

I'm done with death.
Someone comes alongside and talks to me
as I walk. I like her pretty
summer blouse, the white
simplicity of cotton, tiny fine
embroidered flowers.
Only this morning, I was listening
to an organ in a cathedral
in Riga, on a tape sent
from Germany.
Beloved Barbara Crow, it starts out,
this thin ribbon of treasures
sent through air to me
here where

I take
all of it, wholly
into me the way
bits and pieces
of a life
come back, the whole
healed flesh
pressed
over sand and rock.

Earlier today, in the art museum,
I stopped the elevator because
I caught a glimpse of a statue under glass
in the corridor and I thought
it was the seal-woman
I touched once in Winnipeg,
a carving in soapstone of an
Inuit woman with
a child on one side
and a seal on the other, all so meshed
that each was
a part of the other. I want
that seal-woman
the way I want
Sam Hamill's words,
and the elusive,
far-off sounds
of the organ
from Riga,
and birds
rising,
tearing up
from stone,
marking
a new frail
way through sky.

Woman, Child, and Seal
MARY EZEKIEL

photo by William Lubitz

April Morning

They've been rushing
through air all morning—

these geese returning home.
I hear them

again and again,
and drag myself

to the patio.
Chores cast aside,

white cloth
stitched,

stretched,
I'm on my toes,

leaning
out the wooden door,

ready.

SIGNALS

Something is moving on leaden feet
through the garden tonight.

Earlier, when I went out,
it was like an amphitheater

of dark silk, a bowl,
a holding-pen. I could almost

feel a warm cluster of cells
rising up, taking shape.

There were clear
signals

from the underground
of something coming up

for light and air,
forming a pattern

and going on.
Every day,

I look for you.
Like God,

I find you
everywhere.

About the author

Barbara Crow was born and educated in New Zealand, where she worked as a journalist. She met her husband, Jay, in Christchurch on his return from Antarctica, where he'd wintered over as Medical Officer at Byrd Station. They were married in Japan, and their first child, Jonathan, was born in Sasebo. They've lived in New Zealand, in several places throughout the States — including North Carolina, Texas, and Colorado — and are now settled with their youngest daughter, Liz, in Grand Forks, North Dakota.

Ms. Crow's poems have been published in *Landfall*, *Red Weather*, *Dust and Fire*, *Women's Stories Must Be Told*, *Half Tones to Jubilee*, *Poets On*, and *Clearing Space*. She was one of four women poets published in *A Circle of Four* (Dacotah Territory Press, 1989). Her poem "Hands," won first prize in the Fourth Annual *Half Tones to Jubilee* Poetry Contest in 1992.

About the cover artist

The cover of *Coming Up for Light and Air* features a painting on silk, entitled *Zhao Bing of the Later Han*, by an anonymous Chinese artist circa. 1750. The work is one of sixteen paintings in an album entitled *Keepsake from the Cloud Gallery* held now in the collection of the British Library.

Zhao Bing of the Later Han (25-220 A. D.) used to enjoy travel. He could turn water into wine and floated across rivers on a mat, blown by the wind. He could make the dried root of a tree sprout flowers and leaves by placing a speck of cinnabar on it.